D0417225

A CRUISE ALONG THE
MANCHESTER
SHIP CANAL

LANCASHIRE COUNTY LIBRARY

3011811976647 9	
HJ	15-Jul-2010
	£5.99

© The Bluecoat Press 2010

Published by The Bluecoat Press, Liverpool
Book design by March Design, Liverpool
Printed by Kent Valley Colour Printers (Kendal)

Acknowledgements
Thanks to Helen Evans and Mersey Ferries. Photographs from the Manchester Ship Canal
archive were supplied by Manchester County Records Office, with additional images from
Peel Holdings, Ron Davies, Colin McPherson and Alan Novelli.

Cover: The Mersey from Runcorn Bridge.
Artist, Norman Wilkinson (Science and Society Picture Library).
Cover design, Daniel Bickerton.

ISBN 9781904438922

All rights reserved. No part of this publication may be reproduced, stored in a retrieval
system, or transmitted in any form or by any means, electronic, mechanical, photocopying,
recording or otherwise, without prior permission from the publisher.

A CRUISE ALONG THE MANCHESTER SHIP CANAL

Colin Wilkinson

The Bluecoat Press

George's Dock, Liverpool, 1875. Liverpool was at its economic height and the docks were lined with ships from all over the world. George's Dock was filled in during the first years of the twentieth century and the reclaimed land used to build the Pier Head buildings of today.

Liverpool

During the last sixty years, Liverpool has not only increased its population fivefold, but has itself been improved perhaps more than any town in England. It now has as handsome streets, as substantial dwellings and as sumptuous public buildings as any city in the Kingdom. Morton's Railway Guide, 1879

By the 1880s, Liverpool was at its height, a port of world renown. The second city of the British Empire, it was one of the great crossroads of international trade, particularly the Atlantic routes to the Americas. Emigrants had flocked to the city from across Europe: the poor Irish, Welsh and Scots looking for a better life than hardship on the land, gave Liverpool its distinctive Celtic character. From further afield, Italians, Greeks, Scandinavians and Russian Jews amongst many other nationalities, laid down roots with their compatriots and added to the multi-cultural mix that filled the terraced streets and courts to bursting point.

Liverpool's rise and rise had been sudden yet carefully won. Offering lower tariffs than other ports, especially Bristol, it had taken an immense financial risk in building the world's first commercial enclosed wet dock in 1715. By the end of the century, four new wet docks had been added and Liverpool was handling one-sixth of all tonnage from English ports.

The astonishing growth of manufacturing in the North demanded raw materials and Liverpool obliged by importing cotton, tobacco, sugar and all other necessities and then profited again from exporting the finished goods to the world. In 1785, only five bags of American cotton were imported but, by 1837, this had risen to over one million. Liverpool, short of fresh water, never established a textile industry but Manchester, some 30 miles to the east, was ideally placed and had become the centre of a massive industry which drew in satellite towns as far north as Burnley, Colne and Nelson.

The entrepreneurial spirit driving both Liverpool and Manchester manifested itself in finding solutions to the great problem of communications. The road network was totally unsuitable for bulk transport so a network of canals was pioneered to bring goods in and out of the docks and manufacturing centres. When the canal system became stretched to its limits - sometimes cargo took longer to travel from Liverpool to Manchester than it had taken to cross the Atlantic - a revolutionary transport system was financed – the world's first public railway, connecting the two towns and propelling them into an even more remarkable economic cycle.

Enormous wealth was being created and this was reflected in the great public buildings, the parks, churches and other symbols of an aspiring city. In particular, the greatest source of wonder to a stranger was the miles of docks with their fortress-like warehouses and the commercial buildings that handled the insuring, financing and other requirements of a booming port. Liverpool always was a commercial town; it left most of the dirty work of manufacturing to its neighbours.

St George's Hall c1890. The Hall was opened in 1856 as a concert hall and assize courts. Regarded as one of the finest Neo-Classical buildings in the world, it was a statement of Liverpool's confidence as a leader in commerce and culture.

Manchester Town Hall c1880. Anything Liverpool could do, Manchester could match. The Town Hall opened in 1877 and is one of the great buildings of the Gothic Revival. An immense symbol of civic ambition, its commission demanded a building 'equal if not superior, to any similar building in the country' at any cost 'which may be reasonably required.' Somewhat ironically, they chose Liverpool-born, Alfred Waterhouse, as the architect.

Manchester

They (the rich) are powerful … the life of the head of an industrial or commercial house can be compared to that of a princeling. They have the capital sums, the large aims, the responsibilities and dangers, the importance and the pride of a potentate. The warehouses of finished cotton goods and other fabrics are Babylonian monuments. One of them is two hundred yards long and the bales are handled by steam-driven machinery. A cotton mill may contain as many as three hundred thousand spindles.
Hippolyte Taine (1859)

Manchester has a longer history than Liverpool, going back to the Romans, but it was cotton that formed the foundation of its wealth. Its textile industry had developed along traditional lines, resembling that of small towns across Europe. Water was essential to drive the mills and supply the dye houses and the rivers Irwell, Medlock and Irk were lined with workshops. As demand for finished goods grew and new inventions were introduced to speed up the spinning and weaving, so did the size of the factories, to the extent that one mill could produce more in one week than a business in Florence could in one year.

The industrialist was reshaping the landscape, creating the world's greatest industrial city, a wonder to all that beheld it. To some, like the German architect Schinkel, it was a fearful place, *"monstrous masses of red brick built by mere foremen without any trace of architecture"* but to Benjamin Disraeli, it was *"the most wonderful city of modern times"* with its *"illuminated factories with more windows than Italian palaces, and smoking chimneys taller than Italian obelisks"*.

Like Liverpool's rich merchants, Manchester's industrialists were driven by a greater vision than mere wealth. They saw in themselves the qualities of the movers and shapers of the Italian Renaissance, creating a city state in which art flourished alongside commercial success. In both cities, this shared purpose manifested itself in the patronage of art galleries, museums and other great civic ventures. The architecture, indeed, reflected this passion for the Renaissance, adopting its own hybrid Gothic style, typified by such magnificent buildings as Manchester Town Hall and the Royal Exchange.

In fact, Manchester became a victim of its own success to some degree, as demand for land pushed rents ever higher, forcing many mills out to surrounding towns but the businessmen were, as ever, prepared to react to change and they turned their attention to an issue that had vexed them for decades – the cost of transporting goods through Liverpool. It was said that the port charges and punitive railway costs of transporting goods the 30 plus miles to and from Liverpool were greater than for the journey across the Atlantic. Liverpool held a monopoly and Manchester was determined to find a way around it.

THE ROYAL EXCHANGE.

Royal Exchange c1890. When built in 1874, this was one of the largest commodity exchanges in the world, an acknowledgement of Manchester's importance in world markets.

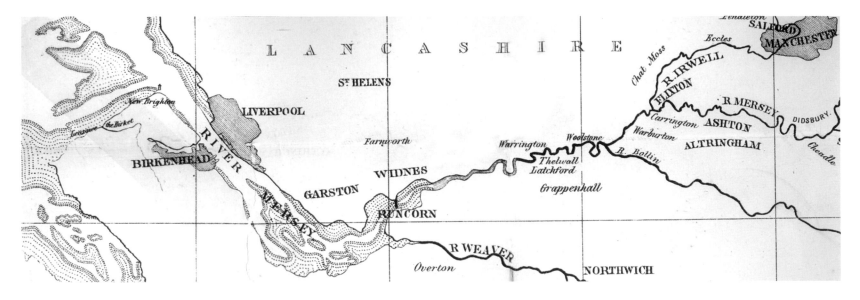

Above. The River Mersey in 1870 showing the problems of navigating beyond Warrington. Not only does the river narrow but it also meanders, almost turning back on itself in places. Even small craft had problems when river levels dropped, particularly in summer months.

Below. The initial plan for the Canal was to use the Mersey for much of the route. By deepening channels and straightening bends, it was hoped a direct route would be possible. However, objections from the Mersey Docks company that it would change the flow of the river as well as the necessary dislocation to established industry along the river made the plan impractical. This plan of 1883 had to be reworked and re-routed through Eastham.

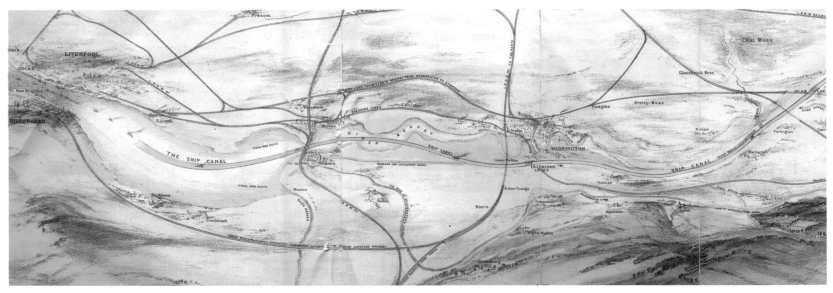

The first steps

The idea of linking Manchester to the sea was not an overnight thought. The Irwell and Mersey had been navigable to some extent by small craft and attempts had been made at different times to dredge the shallows and straighten bends but to no great success. Beyond Warrington, the river meanders and loops back on itself, making it impossible for large craft to navigate.

The introduction of canals such as the Bridgewater Canal and the Mersey and Weaver Navigation made it possible for narrowboats to carry relatively heavy weights to and from Liverpool but they were too slow for the demands of industrialists who wanted their raw materials yesterday.

Suggestions for a canal to Manchester included one from the River Dee as early as 1824 and attempts were made to develop the Bridgewater Canal and to build a new canal linking Manchester to the Mersey but the opening of the Manchester to Liverpool Railway and the subsequent boom in railway building scuppered all attempts to raise finance.

The pressure to build a canal did not go away. By the 1870s, Manchester was facing increased competition from other countries, in particular Germany and the United States. Cutting costs of importing and exporting took an even greater priority and a new scheme surfaced in 1877 with a proposal to excavate a canal to take ocean-going ships. The excitement generated by the successful completion of the Suez Canal in 1867 had raised expectations of what was possible and, in Germany, the government had commenced the construction of the Kiel Canal.

What was required was leadership and a suitable candidate emerged, in 1882, in the shape of Daniel Adamson, an engineer with an international reputation. Bringing together some seventy prominent citizens at his Manchester home, Adamson outlined his plans for a canal which, he considered, would be an easier task than the construction of the Suez Canal. There was some scepticism but the overall effect was to galvanise his audience with the boldness of his vision. The first step had been taken.

Press reaction was mixed, from amusement ('Manchester-sur-Mer' in *Punch*) to a more fearful editorial in a Liverpool newspaper which foresaw the 'complete annihilation of Liverpool'. There were some grounds for the latter view for, by 1880, almost one-third of foreign trade in the United Kingdom passed through Liverpool. Any significant loss of that trade would inevitably damage the city's economic welfare. Liverpool's fears were dealt a further blow when Sir William Fairbairn, another engineer of world repute, boldly stated that once the canal was built, Manchester would 'quadruple her population and render her the first, as well as the most enterprising, city of Europe.'

The argument for a canal had been roundly won, a committee was formed and a scheme proposed which accounted for all the technical problems. An engineer, Leader Williams, was appointed to oversee the plans and negotiations began to push the necessary legislation through Parliament and to acquire the land through which the Canal would be constructed.

At its third attempt, the Ship Canal Bill was finally passed in 1885 amidst tumultuous celebrations in Manchester. The opposition of the Mersey Dock Board, the Corporation of Liverpool and the rail companies had failed, although concessions were made to prevent any changes to the course of the Mersey that might result in the silting of Liverpool's docks. Money had been slow coming in but, once Lord Egerton had replaced Daniel Adamson as chairman, sufficient funds were raised to start the great project.

River Mersey at Statham c.1880. The tranquillity of this river scene at Statham, near Lymm, was about to be shattered as plans for the Ship Canal proceeded at great pace.

The mammoth undertaking gets underway with the building of the first locks at Eastham.

The Big Ditch

The contract to undertake the work was awarded to Thomas Walker, an engineer who had constructed the Severn Tunnel and the first sod was cut at Eastham on 11 November 1887.

In the first year, work progressed without major hitches, with construction commencing in eight sections, but in 1889 a series of disasters befell the enterprise, starting with torrential rain in January which flooded the Latchford section between Thelwall and Lymm washing machinery away and destroying embankments. In the same month, two railway locomotives collided, killing three workmen.

These disasters were followed by protracted litigation from Mersey Docks and Harbour Company regarding possible changes to the scouring effect of the River Mersey and, in November, the rains returned, flooding a six-mile section. To top a difficult year, Thomas Walker died, throwing up legal arguments about the execution of the contract.

In addition to the physical and legal challenges, money was a constant issue as the original estimates of cost were already proving insufficient. With so much invested in the success of the project, it was no time for second thoughts and Manchester Corporation pitched in with loans of £5 million. Money was in place, with the final cost nearly £6 million more than originally estimated.

One of the additional expenses was the decision of Thomas Walker to use mechanical excavators wherever possible, Historically, canals had been dug out by hand by armies of 'navvies' (or navigators) but technical progress meant that machines now presented a more efficient option. Nevertheless, a large number of men was still required to lay down railway lines, install locks, shift earth and dig where the 'steam navvies', as the machines were known, were unable to operate.

The construction at Runcorn in progress, with piles being hammered into the river bed to separate the Canal from the Mersey. The railway bridge is in the background.

A mechanical dredger. It was realised from the start that mechanisation was essential and magnificent machines such as this one were designed to shift millions of feet of earth.

The Navvies

The history of these human 'navvies' is one of the great stories of the construction of the Canal and their heroic endeavours were captured on camera as the work progressed, although the photographs do not show the human cost. Out of a workforce of over 16,000 at its height, over 130 men died through accidents with over 3,000 incidents being treated in the canal's hospital. Although the wages were above average at four and a half pence an hour for a 10-hour day, the work was dangerous with the additional hazards of pneumonia and rheumatism.

Thomas Walker had a great respect for his labour force and built decent huts for the men. He was also one of the first to erect first aid posts at each site with an experienced person in attendance. Injured workers were moved to lighter work and a Liverpool surgeon, Robert Jones, was engaged to operate three site hospitals he had erected along the railway lines.

Although mechanical 'navvies' were essential, the use of human labour was still required in huge numbers. Over 16,000 men were employed in the dangerous work, with frequent injuries and 130 deaths.

A gang of navvies at Acton Grange. The backbreaking work was relatively better paid than other manual work, although it involved living in transit camps alongside the Canal for long periods of time.

Navvies' huts at Acton Grange where families lived during construction.

In the days before the Welfare State, there were few alternatives to work other than the workhouse. Here, a labourer with one arm struggles on to earn a living.

Child labour was a notorious problem in Victorian Britain. Numerous laws were passed restricting its use. Children under ten were forbidden to work underground in the mines in 1842 and other limits on conditions and hours worked in other trades introduced. Nevertheless, it is a shock to see young boys (they look no more than 12) working alongside adults in such demanding work.

A diver prepares to work underwater.

Lunch break.

Noah's Café at Norton. The Canal was mostly some distance from populated areas, so amenities had to be provided on site.

Opposite. Collecting wages.

Drink and food sellers at Mode Wheel, They could make a good living taking their goods to where the men worked.

Travelling salesmen. Workmen would be expected to provide their own clothing out of their own pocket.

Completion and opening

The Ship Canal posed many engineering problems. At its start, at Eastham, the lock gates are opened as the tide rises, so the canal and river rise together. As the tide ebbs, the gates are shut again. To avoid problems with a fast ebb tide, water passes through sluices from the canal to the river at Walton, Runcorn and where the River Weaver meets the Mersey.

In the stretch past Eastham, a solution was found for the disposal of the tons of excavated soil, which were used to create Mount Manisty. The earth was a problem at each section of the canal and the contractor in charge had to decide the most appropriate solution. In the Ellesmere section, Edward Manisty was the contractor and the workers named the large mound of earth in his honour.

Each mile of the canal raised its own problems. Road and rail bridges had to be engineered to minimise disruption. The first swing bridge at Moore Lane has the lowest head-room at only 10ft above the water, with further bridges at Chester Road, Northwich Road and Knutsford Road. Railway viaducts presented different problems because they need at least 70-foot clearance, necessitating huge embankments.

A ship works its way up the Canal soon after its opening. Mount Manisty is the mound of excavated soil on the left.

The 60ft rise in height from sea level also demanded a solution and this was resolved by a series of locks starting at Latchford Locks, where there is a rise (or fall) of twelve and a half feet, with further locks at Irlam, Barton and the Mode Wheel Locks at Salford Docks. An additional problem at Barton was how to deal with the Barton Aqueduct, which carried the Bridgewater Canal over the River Irwell. The solution was a unique swing bridge which carried a tank of water 18ft wide and 7ft deep. The tank's entry and exit could be sealed and the bridge then swung out by hydraulic power to allow ships on the Ship Canal to pass through.

At last, after just over six years of construction, the Canal was completed and a ceremonial procession of boats left Eastham on 1 January 1894, to celebrate one of the greatest feats of engineering of the nineteenth century. The final cost of £14,347,891 entailed a huge risk for those who had underwritten it but Manchester was now officially a port for customs purposes and, once the celebrations were over, could get down to the serious business of making money. By the time Queen Victoria performed the official opening on 21 May, the Canal was well and truly in operation.

The Runcorn Transporter Bridge was constructed in 1905, after the Canal had opened. The Canal restricted the use of ancient ferries and it became necessary to find an efficient means of crossing the river for vehicles and people. A conventional bridge was ruled out as too expensive and a compromise was reached with this structure which would not impede Canal traffic. Never cost-effective, it was eventually replaced by the current road bridge in 1961.

Among the many engineering problems faced, the crossing-point of the Bridgewater Canal was particularly difficult. The solution was to enclose a section of the canal in a tank which could be swung over to allow Ship Canal traffic through. The Barton Swing Aqueduct weighs 1450 tons, of which 800 tons is water.

A Board of Trade inspection at the Irwell Viaduct, 1893. Ten locomotives weighing 750 tons test the strength of the bridge.

A party of dignitaries aboard *SS Fairy Queen* on opening day in 1894.

MANCHESTER SHIP CANAL.   CANAL AT MANCHESTER
OPENING JANUARY 1ST 1894.   [S.S. HELVETIA]   P&S 860   LOOKING TOWARDS SALFORD DOCKS.

The opening ceremony, January 1894. A flotilla of boats sails along the Canal in celebration.

The rise of the Port of Manchester

The opening of the Canal did not immediately usher in a golden age of prosperity. Competition from abroad, particularly Germany and the United States, had hit Liverpool and London hard and its merchants were unhappy at the prospect of losing further trade to the new artery to Manchester. Ganging together, the shipping lines were able to restrict Manchester's access to the Asian markets, particularly India and China, and, until 1895, the cotton market of the southern states of the USA.

They had less success with the short-sea trade, and services to the Baltic, Spain and France began to prosper. In fact, it was to take a decade before the Canal could welcome ships from Australia (in 1904) and New Zealand (1906), thanks to the monopoly of London in that trade, and services to South Africa were only introduced in 1924. Remarkably it took two world wars before ships from the West Indies (1947) and West Africa (1958) began using the Port of Manchester.

The opposition of the railways also hindered the success of the Canal. Acting in defence of their own interests, the companies delayed completing the main link to Salford docks until 1898, isolating the new Port from all inland communications controlled by them. In a further act of hostility, Mersey Docks and Harbour Board dredged the Mersey bar and extended its accommodation for cattle and timber and other trades threatened by Manchester.

A train crosses the Trafford Railway Swing Bridge in the early 1900s.

Faced with such opposition, Manchester had to react and did so by forming its own shipping line, Manchester Liners Ltd. The line proved an immediate success and in 1899 seven cargo vessels were ordered from North East shipyards to suit the Canal (with telescopic topmasts). The order did not go completely to plan as the government conscripted three of the ships as transport for the South African War but, at last, the port was connected to many of the world's trade routes. It had taken time, but Manchester's time was about to begin.

The Canal Company realised quickly that Manchester could never compete with Liverpool for the passenger trade and concentrated instead on general cargo vessels. It had overcome intense opposition from formidable opponents but it had achieved its original objective, to reduce the cost of cargo-handling and ensure the city's competitiveness. What it had not taken into account were the spin-offs the Canal brought, in particular the world's first industrial estate at Trafford Park, on the banks of the Canal, and the boom in manufacturing, particularly in engineering, that was a joint result of the Canal and industrial park. Trafford Park was the early twentieth century equivalent of Silicon Valley – a concentration of skills and technology that was almost without rival.

Discharging timber at the newly opened Manchester Docks.

Two photographs of the Canal illustrating the remarkable achievement of creating an inland port capable of taking ocean-going ships.

The Canal today

The demise of the Port of Manchester did not signal the end of the Ship Canal. Far from it. The purchase of the Canal and the redundant Manchester Docks by Peel Holdings in 1987 was followed by the purchase of Mersey Docks and Harbour Company in 2005. After all the past history of rivalry and competition, Manchester and Liverpool were brought together under the same umbrella. Peel's ambitions were in keeping with the great nineteenth century entrepreneurs who had created the two great cities of the Industrial Revolution. Far from buying redundant docks and waterways, they were determined to respond to changes in world trade that would give a future to the region.

The most ambitious plan is their Ocean Gateway scheme which aims to transform the economic prospects along the Mersey and Manchester Ship Canal. At the western end, new twenty-first century riverfronts of skyscrapers will face each other at Birkenhead and Liverpool. In Salford, the old dock areas have already been converted to mixed uses, including the iconic buildings of the Lowry Gallery, Imperial War Museum North and MediaCity at Salford Quays. The Canal is being revitalised for goods transport and Tesco has become the first supermarket to start transporting goods using super-barges from Liverpool to the container terminal at Irlam, saving the need to use hundreds of lorries.

The Manchester Ship Canal was a 'superhighway' of the early twentieth century. Peel see its regeneration in the twenty-first century in similar terms, connecting both Liverpool and Manchester to the world through world-class facilities and a dynamic business environment which maximises the value of the Canal, with new housing, industry and attractions to add to its original function of transporting goods.

The stunning transformation of Manchester Docks. The Lowry, designed by Michael Wilford, opened in 2000 as a concert and exhibition venue. It houses a permanent collection of the work of LS Lowry and is a key element of the new waterfront.

Map showing the
course of the
Manchester Ship Canal
from Eastham Locks to
Salford Quays.

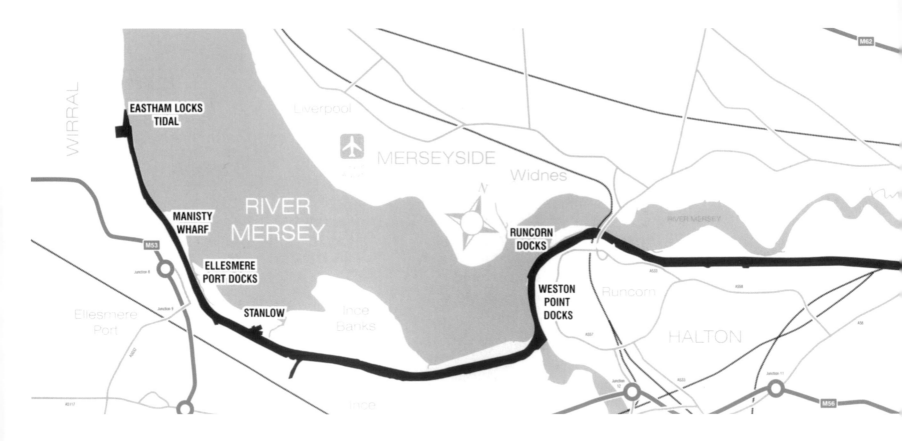

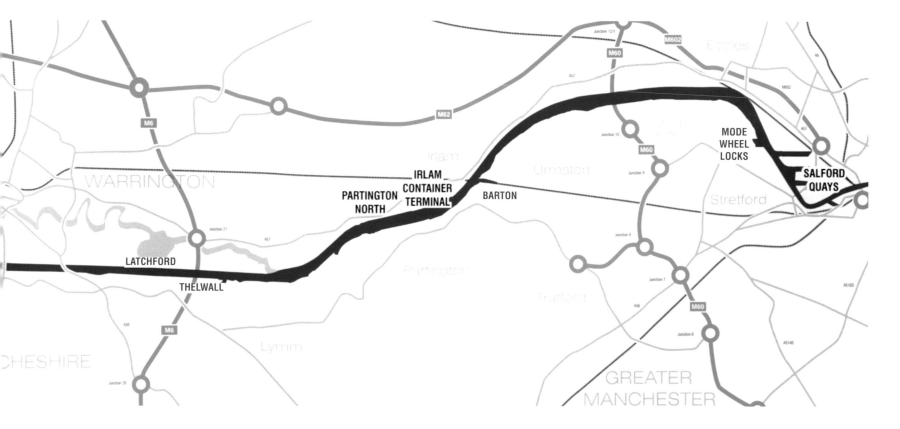

MODE WHEEL LOCKS

SALFORD QUAYS

IRLAM CONTAINER TERMINAL

PARTINGTON NORTH

BARTON

LATCHFORD

THELWALL

A Mersey ferry in mid-Mersey, photographed with the Royal Liver Building in the foreground.
(Photo Ron Davies)

Opposite. The new Liverpool waterfront, with the Museum of Liverpool to the right of the Pier Head buildings and new Mersey Ferries terminal.
(Photo Ron Davies)

A cruise along the Canal

The starting point for any cruise is the Mersey and there can be no more impressive sight than Liverpool's Pier Head. It is only from the river that one can fully appreciate the historical importance of Liverpool, with docks stretching for miles on either side.

The South Docks ceased to function from the 1960s but the quaysides are still there, in particular, the massive bulk of the Albert Dock.

The Canal is entered at Eastham Locks, just past the old, now demolished, ferry landing stage at Eastham. Eastham and its surrounding countryside was a favourite day out for Liverpool city-dwellers in the late nineteenth and early twentieth century.

Eastham has four entry locks. Two are for larger ships, the third for smaller craft (to save water) and the final lock is for tanker access to the Queen Elizabeth II Oil Terminal. From the locks, the Canal follows the banks of the Mersey with, on the left, Mount Manisty and the thin strip of land that separates the Canal from the Mersey. The Canal then passes the Ellesmere Port container terminal, which services the nearby Vauxhall Motors plant. A particular place of interest to canal enthusiasts is the National Waterways Museum, at the junction with the Shropshire Union Canal, which has the largest collection of canal boats in the world, a working lock and dock workers' cottages. The open air museum provides a glimpse of life during the heyday of our waterways, including steam-driven pumping engines which supplied the power for the hydraulic cranes and capstans around the dock.

The National Waterways Museum, the world's largest collection of historic canal boats. (Photo Alan Novelli)

Opposite. A ship leaves Eastham Locks and heads out to sea.

Runcorn Bridge at night. (Photo Alan Novelli)

Opposite. Guinness is one of many companies still actively using the Canal.

All around are reminders of the industrial importance of the waterway, as the journey continues along the Frodsham Marshes. The next major junction with the River Weaver and the Weaver Navigation reveals the chemical complex of Ineos (previously the ICI Castner Kellner plant) at Weston Point. Salt has been a major industry in Cheshire for centuries and the rich deposits around Northwich played a significant role in the region's ascendancy during the Industrial Revolution.

As the Canal bends round towards Runcorn, it passes the disused lock gates which once joined it to the Bridgewater Canal. Built by Francis Egerton, the third Duke of Bridgewater, to convey coal from his mines at Worsley to the industrial centre of Manchester and beyond, it revolutionised transport and helped launch the golden era of canal building.

One of the most dramatic views soon comes into view, for here is the first crossing point of the Mersey for both rail and road. The rail bridge with its solid, crenellated stonework is dominated by the Silver Jubilee Bridge connecting Widnes and Runcorn. It was opened in 1961 to replace the inefficient and outdated transporter bridge. Built originally as a two lane bridge, the volume of traffic necessitated an increase to four lanes.

From Runcorn to Latchford Locks, just before the Thelwall Viaduct which carries the M6 motorway, the Canal passes under a number of bridges carrying important road and rail routes. The first swing bridge is at Moore Lane, followed by the Acton Grange Railway Viaduct. Four road bridges follow, at Chester Road, Northwich Road, the Latchford High Level Bridge and Knutsford Road Bridge, and one rail bridge at Latchford, before the first set of locks since Eastham, 21 miles back. The Latchford Lock with a rise of 12ft 6in, is on an ancient right of way, and members of the public can cross via the canal gates, taking the path along the lock side.

The ferries head towards Liverpool, having cleared Latchford Lock and the Knutsford Road Swing Bridge.

Opposite. Two crowded Mersey ferries with the Acton Bridge Railway Viaduct in the background (the Northwich Road Swing Bridge is opening to allow them through, with the Chester Road Bridge just behind).

A romantic photograph of the Thelwall Viaduct, which carries the M6 over the Canal. (Photo Alan Novelli)

Opposite. The Thelwall ferry. For a small fee, a boatman will row you across the Canal. Ancient rights of way had to be respected after its construction. The ferries have just cleared Latchford Lock and the Knutsford Road Swing Bridge as they head towards Liverpool. (Photo Colin McPherson)

The Thelwall Viaduct, which carries the M6 over both the Mersey and the Ship Canal, was originally built as a one-bridge six-lane highway, but the volume of road traffic necessitated a second bridge which was built alongside the first, allowing extra lanes for north and south bound traffic.

Just beyond Thelwall is the Warburton High Level Bridge, which carries the B5159 across the Canal. It is a toll bridge, charging a small fee to cross a small stone bridge over the old River Mersey course. An Act of Parliament decreed all crossings of the Canal must be toll free but the de Trafford family, who owned the toll, have continued to charge for the use of the bridge over a dry river bed.

The *Royal Daffodil* cruises under the Irlam Viaduct.

Opposite. The Barton Road Swing Bridge and Barton Swing Aqueduct from above.

From Warburton come two further bridges at Cadishead and Irlam before the sets of locks at Irlam and Barton, which have a joint rise of 31ft.

The Barton High Level Bridge takes the M60 over 80ft above the Canal, the highest bridge along the route. Immediately after, there are two more bridges, the Barton Road Swing Bridge and the unique Barton Swing Aqueduct, which replaced James Brindley's original aqueduct, which carried the Bridgewater Canal across the Mersey and Irwell Navigation. At the time of the Ship Canal's construction, the original aqueduct had to be kept in operation until the new crossing was constructed. The solution was to build a swing bridge with a tank containing water which could be sealed when required and swung open to allow ships through, along the Ship Canal. The weight carried is 1450 tons, of which 800 tons is water. Originally operated by hydraulic power, it now had electric pumps installed.

The Centenary Lift Bridge, at Trafford Road, opened in 1994 to coincide with the Canal's centenary, is raised to allow a ship through. It takes less than a minute for the roadway to be lifted 73ft above the water level. (Photo Albert Novelli)

Opposite. Daniel Libeskind's stunning Imperial War Museum North, at Trafford Park. A fitting end to a memorable cruise along one of the greatest engineering achievements of the nineteenth century.

The Canal now enters its final miles into Salford. The Centenary Lift
Bridge, is the final crossing before it enters Trafford Park and the Mode Wheel
Locks, the last on the Canal with a rise of 13ft. The 60ft climb to Manchester
Docks is now complete and the Canal has reached its ultimate destination.

With the demise of commercial traffic, the facing quaysides at Salford
Quay and Trafford Wharf have now been imaginatively converted to mixed
uses, including offices, housing and retail but it is the two iconic buildings of
the Lowry Centre and Imperial War Museum North that catch the eye. These
magnificent attractions and the completion of MediaCity London are all part
of the ambitious regeneration of the Canal and a lasting tribute to the
foresight and ambition of the Victorian entrepreneurs and engineers who
created a world port 40 miles from the sea.

Passengers aboard a Mersey Ferry enjoying a cruise along the length of this remarkable Canal.

Mersey Ferries run regular trips from Wallasey to Salford and Salford to Wallasey with a fascinating commentary which highlights the many points of interest along the Canal.

For further information about Canal cruises:

www.merseyferries.co.uk